# Animal Q&A

# MONKEYS & APES

**Camilla De La Bédoyère**

WINDMILL
BOOKS ™

New York

Published in 2015 by Windmill Books, An Imprint of Rosen Publishing
29 East 21st Street, New York, NY 10010

US Editor: Joshua Shadowens
Publishing Director: Belinda Gallagher
Creative Director: Jo Cowan
Editorial Director: Rosie McGuire
Editor: Sarah Parkin
Volume Design: Phil Morash
Cover Designer: Jo Cowan
Image Manager: Liberty Newton
Indexer: Gill Lee
Production Manager: Elizabeth Collins
Reprographics: Stephan Davis, Thom Allaway, Lorraine King

All artwork from the Miles Kelly Artwork Bank
**Cover** Kitch Bain/Shutterstock.com
**FLPA** 11 Pete Oxford/Minden Pictures; 16 Cyril Ruoso/Minden Pictures
**iStockphoto.com** 4 Robert Churchill; 22 Matthew Okimi
**Shutterstock.com** 3 javarman; 5 Vladimir Wrangel; 7 Sara Robinson; 12 Vitaly Titov & Maria Sidelnikova; 19 Animal; 20 Mike Price

All other photographs are from: digitalSTOCK, digitalvision, John Foxx, PhotoAlto, PhotoDisc, PhotoEssentials, PhotoPro, Stockbyte

Library of Congress Cataloging-in-Publication Data

De la Bédoyère, Camilla, author.
  Monkeys & apes / by Camilla De La Bédoyère.
     pages cm. — (Animal Q & A)
  Includes index.
  ISBN 978-1-4777-9190-5 (library binding) — ISBN 978-1-4777-9191-2 (pbk.) —
ISBN 978-1-4777-9192-9 (6-pack)
  1. Primates—Miscellanea—Juvenile literature. 2. Monkeys—Miscellanea—Juvenile literature.
3. Apes—Miscellanea—Juvenile literature. I. Title. II. Title: Monkeys and apes.
  QL737.P9D433 2015
  599.8—dc23
                              2014001238

Manufactured in the United States of America

# Contents

What is a primate? 4

Are gorillas scary? 5

Do monkeys and apes have tails? 5

Do primates stay awake
   all night? 6

Do bonobos like to play? 7

Which lemur has a stripy tail? 7

Why do chimps lick sticks? 8

Do chimps like to chatter? 9

Why do monkeys sleep in trees? 9

Do apes love their moms? 10

Why does an aye-aye have
   a long finger? 11

Why do orangutans climb trees? 11

Do primates help forests
   to grow? 12

Why is a slow loris slow? 13

When do monkeys fall out
   of trees? 13

How fast can a gibbon swing? 14

Do monkeys eat crabs? 15

Do primates have hands and
   feet like us? 15

Which monkey is the biggest? 16

Why do chimps pull faces? 17

Which monkey has a mustache? 17

Do monkeys change color? 18

Which ape has a
   colorful backside? 19

Why does a sifaka skip? 19

How big is a gorilla? 20

What is the ugliest monkey? 21

Why do gorillas beat
   their chests? 21

How do monkeys keep warm? 22

Glossary 23

Further Reading 23

Index 24

Websites 24

# what is a primate?

**Monkeys and apes are primates.** They have big brains and are very clever. Most primates are furry. They have hands with thumbs and fingernails. Humans are primates, too.

Spider monkeys

## cry baby!

Bush babies are noisy primates that live in forests. When they make loud calls to each other, They sound like crying babies.

## Spell

How many words can you make using the letters in the word PRIMATE?

## Are gorillas scary?

Gorillas are usually gentle animals. However they can be very fierce if they have to protect their families. Males can die fighting to save their young.

## Do monkeys and apes have tails?

Monkeys have tails, but apes don't. Tails help monkeys to climb and keep their balance. Apes are usually larger than monkeys and they also have bigger brains. Gorillas, chimpanzees (chimps), bonobos, orangutans, gibbons and humans are apes.

Orangutan

5

# Do primates stay awake all night?

**Nocturnal primates do!** Animals that are nocturnal sleep during the day and wake up at sunset. Tarsiers have big eyes to help them see in the dark. They can rotate their heads 180 degrees, so they can see what's behind them.

Tarsier

# Do bonobos like to play?

Bonobos love to play! Some bonobos living in a zoo play their own game of blind man's bluff! They cover their eyes and try to walk without bumping into things.

## Play

Ask a grown-up to help you set up a game of blind man's bluff with your friends.

# Which lemur has a stripy tail?

Ring-tailed lemurs have long, bushy tails with black-and-white stripes. The males have smelly tails, and when they fight they wave them at each other.

Ring-tailed lemur

## Hold tight!

Lemurs run and jump through trees. Babies have to grip tightly to their mothers' fur so they don't fall off!

7

# why do chimps lick sticks?

**Because they get covered with juicy termites!**
Chimps poke sticks into big termite nests. The insects swarm over the sticks, which the chimps then pull out so they can lick up the tasty termites.

Chimps ⟶

8

## Sign

Ask a parent to use the Internet to discover how to sign for "drink" and "thank you."

## Greedy monkey!

Barbary macaques have large cheek pouches. When they find food, they stuff it into their pouches and save it for later.

# Do chimps like to chatter?

Some do! A chimp called Washoe learned how to use sign language to talk. She used her hands to make signs for lots of words, such as "drink" and "food."

Squirrel monkey

# Why do monkeys sleep in trees?

Monkeys can hide in a tree's branches, so they feel safer in trees than on the ground. Animals that want to eat other animals are called predators. The predators of squirrel monkeys include eagles, baboons and prickly porcupines.

# Do apes love their moms?

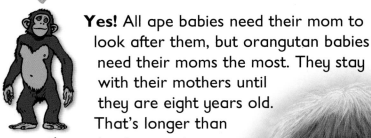

**Yes!** All ape babies need their mom to look after them, but orangutan babies need their moms the most. They stay with their mothers until they are eight years old. That's longer than any other primate, apart from humans.

Orangutan and baby

# why does an aye-aye have a long finger?

An aye-aye has a long finger to get to tasty grubs. These little primates tap trees with their fingers. If they hear a grub moving inside, they make a hole and pull it out with their extra-long middle finger.

Aye-aye

## what a racket!

Some mangabeys make a honk-bark noise. Others whoop to call each other and make a gobble sound to say who they are.

# why do orangutans climb trees?

Orangutans climb trees to play in the branches, to find fruit to eat and to stay safe. Predators such as tigers, leopards and crocodiles hunt orangutans.

## Make

Who looks after you? Make them a beautiful card to say thank you.

11

## Do primates help forests to grow?

**Yes they do!** By eating plants and fruits, primates shape the trees and bushes. They also spread plant seeds in their waste. Primate waste puts nutrients into the soil and helps new plants to grow.

Macaque ⟶

## Why is a slow loris slow?

A slow loris likes to take life at a gentle pace. Moving slowly saves energy, so you don't need to find lots of food. It also helps an animal to stay hidden from predators.

Slow loris

**Race**

Have a slow race with a friend. The last person to finish is the winner!

**Watch out bugs!**

Slow-moving primates can creep up on their prey, such as insects, and pounce at the last second.

## When do monkeys fall out of trees?

When they get too greedy! Bird eggs are a special treat for primates. Smart birds build their nests on slender branches where monkeys can't reach them.

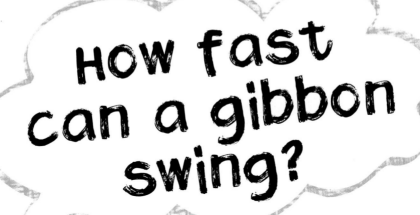

# How fast can a gibbon swing?

**Gibbons move faster than any other primate.** They can swing through trees at great speed — up to 35 miles per hour (56 km/h). Gibbons can cover up to 50 feet (15 m) in just one swing.

Gibbons

Crab-eating macaque

# Do monkeys eat crabs?

Some monkeys will eat almost anything they can find! Crab-eating macaques live in swamps, and they will grab crabs and frogs out of shallow water. Sometimes they just drop into the cool water for a swim.

# Do primates have hands and feet like us?

Instead of paws and claws, primates have fingers, toes and flat fingernails just like us. This means they can grab hold of branches and delicately pinch small things.

## Count

If one macaque can catch five crabs, how many can three macaques catch?

## Super movers!

Spider monkeys are some of the fastest primate climbers. They have very long arms, legs and tails.

# which monkey is the biggest?

**Male mandrills are the world's biggest monkeys.** They are also the most colorful of all furry animals. Mandrills have enormous fangs that can grow to nearly 2.8 inches (7 cm) in length. Males are twice as big as females.

Mandrill

# Why do chimps pull faces?

Chimps pull faces to show how they are feeling. They pout when they want attention, open their lips when they are playful and bare their teeth when they are worried.

## Pout

Try out some chimp faces in front of a mirror. Make an angry face too.

Pouting face

Worried face

Play face

## Go wild!

Beautiful golden tamarins were once popular zoo animals, but now they are being released back into the wild so they can live free.

# Which monkey has a mustache?

Emperor tamarins have big white mustaches. Other tamarins have golden fur, crowns of white hair, beards or hairy ears. Tamarins live in South America.

17

# Do monkeys change color?

**Silvered langurs do!** These monkeys have silver-gray fur, but their babies are born bright orange. After three months, gray fur begins to grow. No one knows why the babies are orange, but it may remind older monkeys to be gentle with them.

Silvered langur

Silvered langur baby →

18

# Which ape has a colorful backside?

A healthy male mandrill baboon has a brightly colored backside. Their bald backsides have blue, pink or lilac skin. Female baboons often have pink or bright red backsides.

## A handy tail!

Monkeys use their tails like an extra arm or leg. They can hang from branches using their tails.

# Why does a sifaka skip?

Skipping is a fast way for sifakas (a type of lemur) to travel. They stand upright, with their arms stretched out, and skip sideways, scooting across the ground. Sifakas stick their tails out so they don't fall over as they hop, bound and leap.

**Imagine**
Pretend to be a sifaka and skip about!

Sifaka

# How big is a gorilla?

**Adult male gorillas are very big.** They are called silverbacks, and they are up to 6 feet (180 cm) in height and weigh about 660 pounds (300 kg). That's the same weight as almost four people!

Silverback gorilla

## Measure

Use a measuring tape to find out how tall a gorilla is.

# What is the ugliest monkey?

Red uakaris (wak-ar-ees) are one of the ugliest monkeys. When they are born, baby uakaris have grey faces, but they turn bright red as they get older.

## Bathtime fun!

Suryia the orangutan lives in a wildlife park. He loved splashing in the bath and was taken to a pool. Suryia can now swim underwater!

↑ Red uakari

# Why do gorillas beat their chests?

When a silverback gorilla stands up and beats his chest, it is time to get away fast! This is his way of warning you that he is getting angry and might attack.

# HOW do monkeys keep warm?

**Most monkeys live in warm places.** Japanese macaques live in mountainous areas where the weather can turn very cold. They keep warm by soaking in pools of hot water that bubble up from the ground.

Japanese macaques

# Glossary

**fangs** (FANGZ) Long, sharp teeth.

**grubs** (GRUBZ) Insects in an early stage of growth.

**Internet** (IN-ter-net) An electronic network that connects computers around the world and provides facts and information.

**nocturnal** (nok-TUR-nul) Active during the night.

**nutrients** (NOO-tree-ents) Food that a living thing needs to live and grow.

**predators** (PREH-duh-terz) Animals that kill other animals for food.

**prey** (PRAY) An animal that is hunted by another animal for food.

**primate** (PRY-mayt) The group of animals that are more advanced than others and includes monkeys, gorillas, and humans.

**zoo** (ZOO) A place where many kinds of animals are kept so that people can see them.

# Further Reading

Niver, Heather Moore. *Chimps and Monkeys Are Not Pets!* When Pets Attack. New York: Gareth Stevens, 2014.

Spilsbury, Richard and Louise Spilsbury. *Chimpanzee Troops.* Animal Armies. New York: PowerKids Press, 2013.

Wood, Alix. *Weird Animals in the Wild.* Earth's Grossest Animals. New York: Windmill Books, 2014.

# Index

**A**
ape(s), 4–5, 10
aye-aye, 11

**B**
baboon(s), 9, 19
birds, 13
bonobos, 5, 7
brains, 4–5

**C**
crocodiles, 11

**E**
eagles, 9
ears, 17
eyes, 6–7

**F**
fangs, 16
fingernails, 4, 15
food, 9, 13
fur, 7, 17–18

**G**
gibbons, 5, 14
gorilla(s), 5, 20–21
grub(s), 11

**H**
humans, 4–5, 10

**I**
insects, 8, 13
Internet, 9

**L**
lemur(s), 7, 19
leopards, 11
lips, 17
loris, 13

**M**
mandrill(s), 16, 19
mustaches, 17

**N**
nests, 8, 13

**O**
orangutan(s), 5, 10–11, 21

**P**
predators, 9, 11, 13
prey, 13

**S**
sifakas, 19

**T**
tamarins, 17
tarsiers, 6
teeth, 17
termite(s), 8
tigers, 11

**W**
waste, 12

**Z**
zoo, 7

# websites

For web resources related to the subject of this book, go to:
www.windmillbooks.com/weblinks and select this book's title.